P9-CLC-009

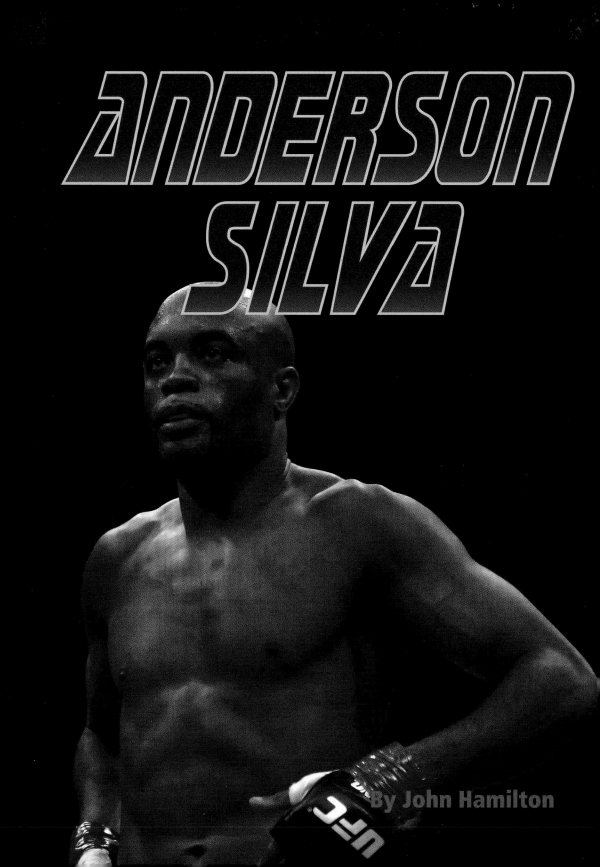

ANDERSON SILVA

By John Hamilton

Published by ABDO Publishing Company, 8000 West 78th Street, Suite 310, Edina, MN 55439. Copyright ©2011 by Abdo Consulting Group, Inc. International copyrights reserved in all countries. No part of this book may be reproduced in any form without written permission from the publisher. A&D Xtreme™ is a trademark and logo of ABDO Publishing Company.

Printed in the United States of America, North Mankato, Minnesota.
052010
092010

Editor: Sue Hamilton
Graphic Design: John Hamilton
Cover Photo: AP Images
Interior Photos: AP Images, p. 1, 2, 3, 6-7, 8-9, 10, 14 (inset), 14-15, 16 (inset), 16-17, 22-23, 23 (inset), 28 (inset), 28-29, 30-31; Getty Images, p. 4-5, 11, 12-13, 18 (inset), 18-19, 24-25, 26 (inset), 26-27, 32.

Library of Congress Cataloging-in-Publication Data

Hamilton, John, 1959-
  Anderson Silva / John Hamilton.
     p. cm. -- (Xtreme UFC)
  Includes index.
  ISBN 978-1-61613-478-5
  1. Silva, Anderson, 1975 Apr. 14---Juvenile literature. 2. Martial artists--Brazil--Biography. 3. Mixed martial arts--Juvenile literature. I. Title.
  GV1113.S57H36 2011
  796.8092--dc22
  [B]
                                    2010018544

CONTENTS

ANDERSON

Anderson Silva is a middleweight mixed martial arts fighter from Brazil. By April, 2010, he held an unbeaten record of 11 straight wins in the Ultimate Fighting Championship (UFC). His nickname is "The Spider." Inside the Octagon, he loves to fight standing up, trading punches and kicks. But he also has crazy ground-and-pound skills.

SILVa

At UFC 101, on August 8, 2009, Silva
fought Forrest Griffin. Silva
knocked Griffin down three
times in the very first round. He
won with a knockout jab to Griffin's face.

Xtreme Fight

FIGHTER

STATS

Name: Anderson Silva

Nickname: The Spider

Born: Curitiba, Brazil, April 14, 1975

Height: 6 feet, 2 inches (1.9 m)

Weight: 185 pounds (84 kg)

Nationality: Brazilian

Division: Middleweight—171 to 185 pounds (78 to 84 kg)

Reach: 77.6 inches (197 cm)

Fighting Style: Brazilian jiu-jitsu, tae kwon do, boxing, Muay Thai kickboxing, judo

Fighting Out Of: Curitiba, Brazil

Martial Arts Rank: Black belts in Brazilian jiu-jitsu, tae kwon do, and judo

Mixed Martial Arts Record (as of April 2010)

　　Total Fights: 30

　　Wins: 26 (15 by knockout, 4 by submission, 7 by decision)

　　Losses: 4

Anderson Silva's UFC Fight Record

Event	Date	Result	Opponent	Method
UFC 112	4/10/2010	Win	Demian Maia	Unanimous Decision
UFC 101	8/8/2009	Win	Forrest Griffin	Knockout
UFC 97	4/18/2009	Win	Thales Leites	Unanimous Decision
UFC 90	10/25/2008	Win	Patrick Côté	Technical Knockout
UFC FN	7/19/2008	Win	James Irvin	Knockout
UFC 82	3/1/2008	Win	Dan Henderson	Submission
UFC 77	10/20/2007	Win	Rich Franklin	Technical Knockout
UFC 73	7/7/2007	Win	Nate Marquardt	Technical Knockout
UFC 67	2/3/2007	Win	Travis Lutter	Submission
UFC 64	10/14/2006	Win	Rich Franklin	Technical Knockout
UFC FN	6/28/2006	Win	Chris Leben	Knockout

FN=*Fight Night*

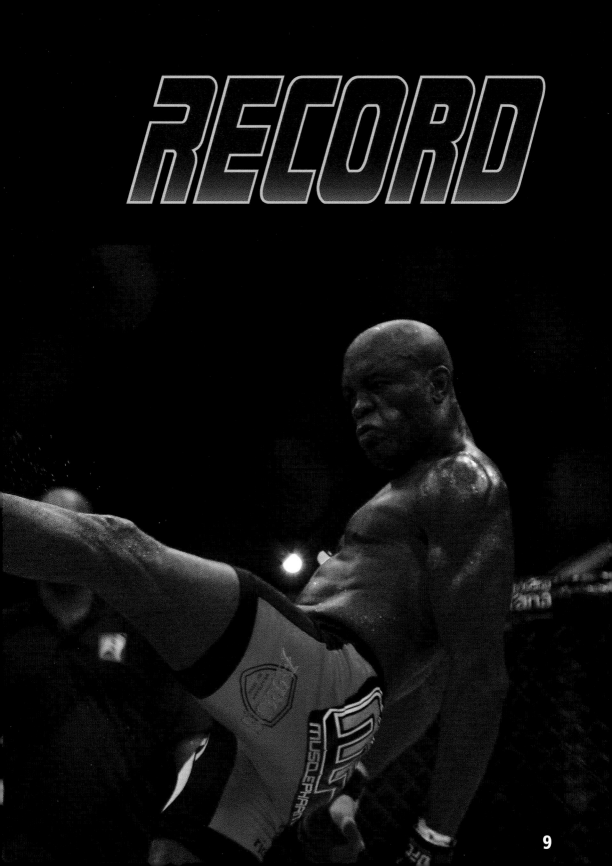

RECORD

EARLY

Anderson Silva started training in tae kwon do at age 14. In his 20s, he fought in mixed martial arts matches in his native Brazil, as well as Japan and other countries. He won his first UFC match in 2006, against Chris Leben, and has been unstoppable ever since.

Xtreme Fact

Anderson Silva trains relentlessly from his hometown of Curitiba, Brazil. He is a master of many styles, with black belts in tae kwon do, Brazilian jiu-jitsu, and judo.

CAREER

After winning his first UFC fight against Chris Leben, Silva squared off against middleweight legend Rich Franklin. Silva beat Franklin less than three minutes into the first round. With the victory, Silva became the new UFC middleweight champion.

HIGHLIGHTS

At UFC 67, on February 3, 2007, Silva defended his middleweight title against jiu-jitsu fighter Travis Lutter. Silva won with a triangle choke submission in the second round.

UFC 73 Vs. Nate Marquardt

At UFC 73 on July 7, 2007, Silva fought Nate Marquardt, an expert in Brazilian jiu-jitsu. But Marquardt was no match for Silva's well-rounded martial arts skills. Silva won the match at the end of the first round, with a technical knockout.

UFC 77 Vs. Rich Franklin

On October 20, 2007, Silva fought a rematch against former middleweight champion Rich Franklin, who badly wanted his title back. Silva denied Franklin the honor, defeating him once again, this time with a technical knockout in the second round.

UFC Fight Night: Silva vs. Irvin

On July 19, 2008, Silva moved up to the light heavyweight division to fight James Irvin. About one minute into the first round, Silva caught one of Irvin's kicks and then knocked him to the canvas. After a barrage of follow-up punches, Silva was declared the winner by knockout.

UFC 90 Vs. Patrick Côté

On October 25, 2008, Silva defended his middleweight title against Patrick Côté, a mixed martial artist from Canada. Côté became Silva's first UFC opponent to make it into the third round. But after a knee injury, Côté could not continue. Silva was declared the winner by technical knockout.

UFC 97 Vs. Thales Leites

On April 18, 2009, Silva fought Thales Leites, a fellow jiu-jitsu expert from Brazil. Leites was the first UFC fighter to ever go five full rounds with Silva. But when the judges gave their decision, Silva once again came out on top.

UFC 101 Vs. Forrest Griffin

On August 8, 2009, Silva again moved up to the light heavyweight division. This time he faced dangerous striker and former UFC champion Forrest Griffin. Always a fan favorite, Griffin was expected to do well. But Silva had other ideas in mind.

Knockout Power

Silva knocked Griffin down three times in the very first round. In the last exchange, Silva dodged a flurry of punches. Then he delivered a right-hand jab that sent Griffin to the canvas. Silva was declared the winner by knockout.

UFC 112
Vs. Demian
Maia

On April 10, 2010, Silva dominated Brazilian Demian Maia. It was Silva's 11th straight UFC win. The undefeated champion proved that he may be the best mixed martial artist the sport has ever seen.

Brazilian Jiu-Jitsu
A fighting style made popular by fighters from Brazil that specializes in grappling and ground fighting, including chokes and joint locks.

Decision
If a match finishes without a clear victor, either by knockout or submission, a panel of three judges decides the winner. If only two judges agree on the winner, it is called a split decision.

Ground and Pound
A style of fighting where an opponent is taken down and then punched or submitted.

Jab
A strike used in boxing and karate. When in a fighting stance, the lead fist is thrown straight out. Jabs are not as powerful as regular punches, but they are very quick and effective.

GLOSSARY

Kickboxing
A style of fighting that relies mainly on a mix of kicking and punching. Muay Thai is a type of kickboxing that is the national sport of Thailand.

Mixed Martial Arts
A full-contact sport that allows a mix of different martial arts, such as boxing, karate, and wrestling. The most popular mixed martial arts (MMA) organization is the Ultimate Fighting Championship (UFC).

Octagon
The eight-sided ring in which Ultimate Fighting Championship fighters compete.

Triangle Choke
A ground fighting technique. The defender on the bottom wraps his legs around the attacker's neck and one arm in the shape of a triangle.

INDEX